discovermore

Space Science

Exploring Constellations

Elizabeth Pruet

Britannica Educational Publishing

IN ASSOCIATION WITH

THE ROSEN PUBLISHING GROUP

Published in 2026 by Britannica Educational Publishing (a trademark of Encyclopædia Britannica, Inc.) in association with The Rosen Publishing Group, Inc.
2544 Clinton Street, Buffalo, NY 14224

Distributed exclusively by Rosen Publishing.
To see additional Britannica Educational Publishing titles, go to rosenpublishing.com.

Editor: Danielle Haynes
Book Design: Michael Flynn

Photo Credits: Cover New Africa/Shutterstock.com; (series background) Dai Yim/Shutterstock.com; p. 4 oscargutzo/Shutterstock.com; p. 5 Piotr Sikora/Shutterstock.com; p. 6 https://commons.wikimedia.org/wiki/File:Seal_Hero_fighting_two_winged_deamons-MBA_Lyon_E408-IMG_0087.jpg; p. 7 https://commons.wikimedia.org/wiki/File:-200_Sternenliste_aus_Uruk_star_list_anagoria.JPG; p. 8 pasteque/Shutterstock.com; p. 9 pasteque/Shutterstock.com; p. 10 https://commons.wikimedia.org/wiki/File:Ptolemy_1476_with_armillary_sphere_model.jpg; p. 11 Peter Hermes Furian/Shutterstock.com; p. 13 Ekaterina Karikh/Shutterstock.com; p. 15 (top) George Trumpeter/Shutterstock.com; p. 15 (bottom) Shahrizal MS/Shutterstock.com; p. 16 Alones/Shutterstock.com; p. 17 Mark Rademaker/Shutterstock.com; p. 19 https://commons.wikimedia.org/wiki/File:Constellations,_equirectangular_plot.svg; p. 20 NigelSpiers/Shutterstock.com; p. 21 oxameel/Shutterstock.com; p. 22 Rawpixel.com/Shutterstock.com; p. 23 magr80/Shutterstock.com; p. 24 Rawpixel.com/Shutterstock.com; p. 25 fumimicreative/Shutterstock.com; p. 26 Elena Eskevich/Shutterstock.com; p. 27 Tae PY15MU/Shutterstock.com; p. 29 (top) yoko_ken_chan/Shutterstock.com; p. 29 (bottom) fumimicreative/Shutterstock.com.

Cataloging-in-Publication Data
Names: Pruet, Elizabeth.
Title: Exploring constellations / Elizabeth Pruet.
Description: New York : Britannica Educational Publishing, in association with Rosen Educational Services, 2026. | Series: Discover more: space science | Includes glossary and index.
Identifiers: ISBN 9781641905244 (library bound) | ISBN 9781641905237 (pbk) | ISBN 9781641905251 (ebook)
Subjects: LCSH: Constellations--Juvenile literature. | Stars--Juvenile literature.
Classification: LCC QB802.P78 2026 | DDC 523.8--dc23

Manufactured in the United States of America

CPSIA Compliance Information: Batch #CWBRIT26. For further information contact Rosen Publishing at 1-800-237-9932.

Contents

Stargazing

Stargazing is one of the oldest hobbies among humankind. For thousands of years, people have looked at stars and noticed patterns. Connecting the stars in their minds, people saw imaginary pictures of animals and objects. We call these star patterns **constellations**.

In scientific terms, constellations are not real. The stars in constellations are often very far away from each other and therefore not close enough to form patterns. They appear close together only to viewers on Earth.

Modern humans can use telescopes to look at the stars and planets in the sky, but constellations are more easily seen by the naked eye.

Sailors would have used this star map from 1891 to navigate the oceans.

Constellations are like a map, making it an easy way for scientists to locate certain stars in the sky. They have also been used for navigation on land and at sea for ages. Many cultures have built legends and stories around constellations, giving them special meaning. These constellations often have different names linked to these stories.

WORD WISE

THE WORD "CONSTELLATION" COMES FROM TWO LATIN WORDS: *CON*, MEANING "WITH," AND *STELLA*, MEANING "STAR."

The Ancient Mesopotamians

Some of the earliest nomads to settle into sedentary civilizations did so in an area called Mesopotamia. The Sumerians settled what is now Iraq in about 3300 BCE. It was there that the first civilizations were formed. Historians think they also were the first people who named star patterns in the sky. Historians believe that the Sumerians named the constellations after the animals living around them, such as bulls, rams, and lions.

The art of ancient Mesopotamian cultures, such as the engraving on this cylinder seal, often features stars and other objects of the night sky.

This cuneiform tablet from around 320–150 BC lists the various constellations used by the ancient Babylonians in modern-day Iraq.

The Sumerians kept written records by drawing pictures on clay tablets, writing in a system called cuneiform. They recorded their observations about the sun, moon, and other bodies in the sky. Their records and legends were passed on to later civilizations that settled in the same area, including the Akkadians, Assyrians, and Babylonians.

Consider This

Imagine you lived in ancient Mesopotamia. Would you keep a record of what you saw in the sky?

The Ancient Greeks

While the Mesopotamians were the first to identify constellations, the ancient Greeks kept more detailed records of what they observed. Beginning around the fourth century BCE, ancient Greek astronomers began keeping lists of constellations, building on the knowledge of the Mesopotamians. Some kept the same original animal names, only translated into Greek or Latin. For example, the Babylonian constellation Mul Ur Gu La was renamed Leo in Greek. Both names mean "lion."

Leo is one of the most visible constellations on Earth because it lines up with the planet's equator.

The constellation Sagittarius, which has 17 named stars, has its roots in the Sumerian civilization.

The Greeks tied legends and **myths** from their culture to constellations. According to legend, the god Zeus placed the constellation Delphinus, the dolphin, in the sky to honor the dolphin that saved a famous Greek poet from drowning. The constellation Sagittarius, meanwhile, is meant to be a centaur—a creature that is half human, half horse.

WORD WISE

A MYTH IS A STORY THAT EXPLAINS HOW THINGS CAME TO BE. IN ANCIENT GREECE, MYTHS USUALLY INVOLVED GODS.

Ptolemy's Almagest

One of the most important scientific figures in ancient times was the Greek Ptolemy (TOH-luh-me), who lived in Egypt. He wrote a series of books about the contents of the sky called the *Almagest.*

Divided into 13 books, the work included a plan of the solar system, mathematical ideas, and information on celestial objects such as the moon, sun, and stars.

Ptolemy's ideas about the universe were important to scientists for hundreds of years.

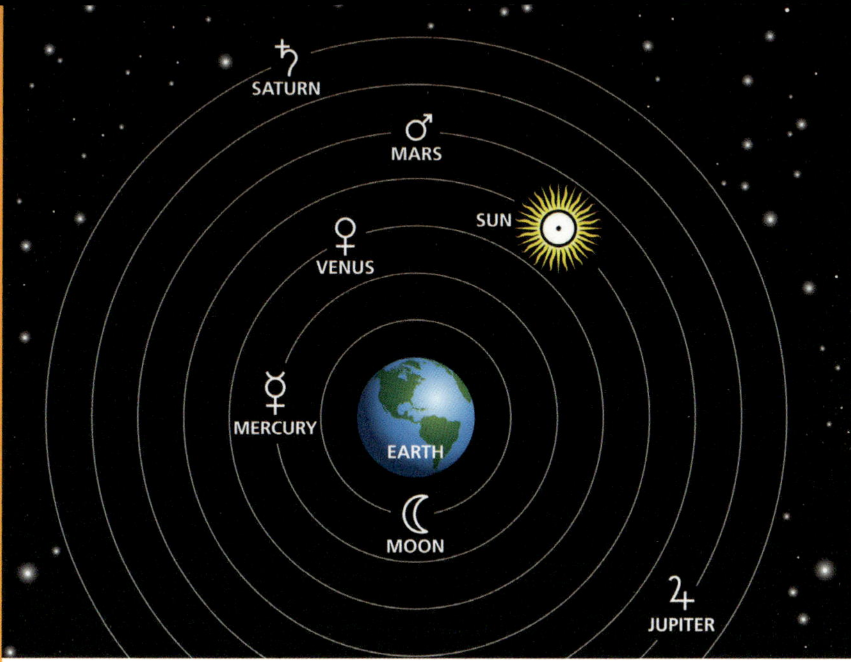

Unfortunately, not all of Ptolemy's theories were correct. He believed the Earth was the center of the universe, and all other planets and the sun orbit around it.

Ptolemy listed 48 constellations, all of which are still recognized today. His list was not perfect or complete. It included only the constellations he could see from his part of the world. The work was translated into Arabic and Latin, and it was the main guide for astronomers for many centuries. Unfortunately, this meant many people believed for years that the sun and planets in our solar system revolved around Earth. This is what's called a geocentric view of the universe.

Consider This

Why was it important for Ptolemy to create his list? How did it help future astronomers?

The Zodiac Constellations

Many of Ptolemy's constellations are still considered official today. Twelve of them had extra-special meaning. These have become the zodiac, or circle of animals. The constellations of the zodiac are positioned in a ring around Earth. Ancient Greeks and Romans tracked the movement of these constellations through the sky based on where they were in relation to the sun. They recorded the dates that these constellations were due to appear.

There are detailed legends about each constellation in the zodiac. For example, Gemini refers to the twins Castor and Pollux. When Castor was killed in battle, Pollux was so upset that the god Zeus transformed the two brothers into the Gemini constellation so they could be together.

Consider This

Some people believe that the constellations of the zodiac affect how people act and what their futures will be.

Each sign of the zodiac is represented by a different constellation and a symbol.

Maps of the Sky

Constellations aren't just about imagining pretty pictures in the sky or telling stories. They have a variety of practical uses, too. Before there were calendars, farmers could tell when the seasons would change by how and where constellations appeared in the sky.

Constellations are also useful for navigation. A group of stars called the Big Dipper, in the constellation Ursa Major, points to the star called Polaris, or the North Star. Early navigators learned to use the position of Polaris to find their way as they traveled. They used tools such as the astrolabe or sextant to measure the distance of stars from the horizon to figure out their location.

Ancient farmers knew that when the constellation Orion was fully visible in the sky that winter was coming soon.

compare and contrast

How do stars compare to an electronic navigation device, such as GPS? What are the strengths and weaknesses of each method?

Many ships keep an early navigation device called a sextant as backup in case more modern technology fails.

Astronomers also use constellations for practical reasons. They use them to locate where other objects in space can be found. Although each constellation has stars that make up its shape, any star located within that pattern is part of the constellation. Saying that a star is in a constellation is a simple way to explain that star's location.

The Big Dipper—also known as Ursa Major—has seven bright stars that make up its primary design. However, all the other stars you can see in or around the Big Dipper are also considered part of it.

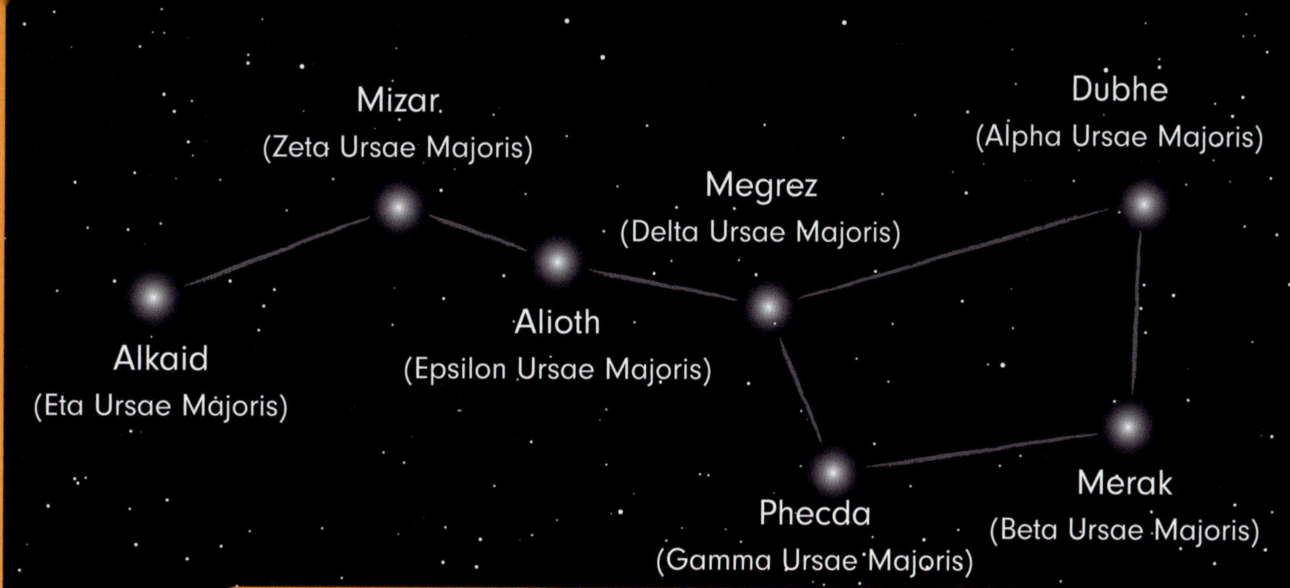

In the Big Dipper, the stars are designated by a letter from the Greek alphabet starting at the top right corner (Dubhe is alpha) and ending at the tip of the handle (Alkaid is eta).

Stars have names according to the constellation in which they are found. The brightest stars in a constellation are named with Greek letters comparing them to other stars in the constellation. For example, the seven brightest stars in the Big Dipper are named after the first seven letters of the Greek alphabet—alpha, beta, gamma, delta, epsilon, zeta, and eta.

Consider This

Does it make sense to use constellations to locate objects in the sky, even though there is no scientific reason for doing so?

Modern Constellations

The number of constellations has varied over time and throughout cultures. Ptolemy's list of constellations was limited by what he himself could observe. Over time, more constellations were named as they were observed from different parts of the world.

Scientists did not always agree on which star groups were official constellations. But in the 20th century, astronomers around the world shared information to create a complete list of constellations, which included those described by Ptolemy.

A group called the International Astronomical Union, or the IAU, created this official list in 1922. They chose the constellations that were most commonly known at the time. Today's list includes 88 constellations named after characters and creatures from myths, as well as animals and objects. One constellation, Vela, is even named after the Latin word for the sails of a ship.

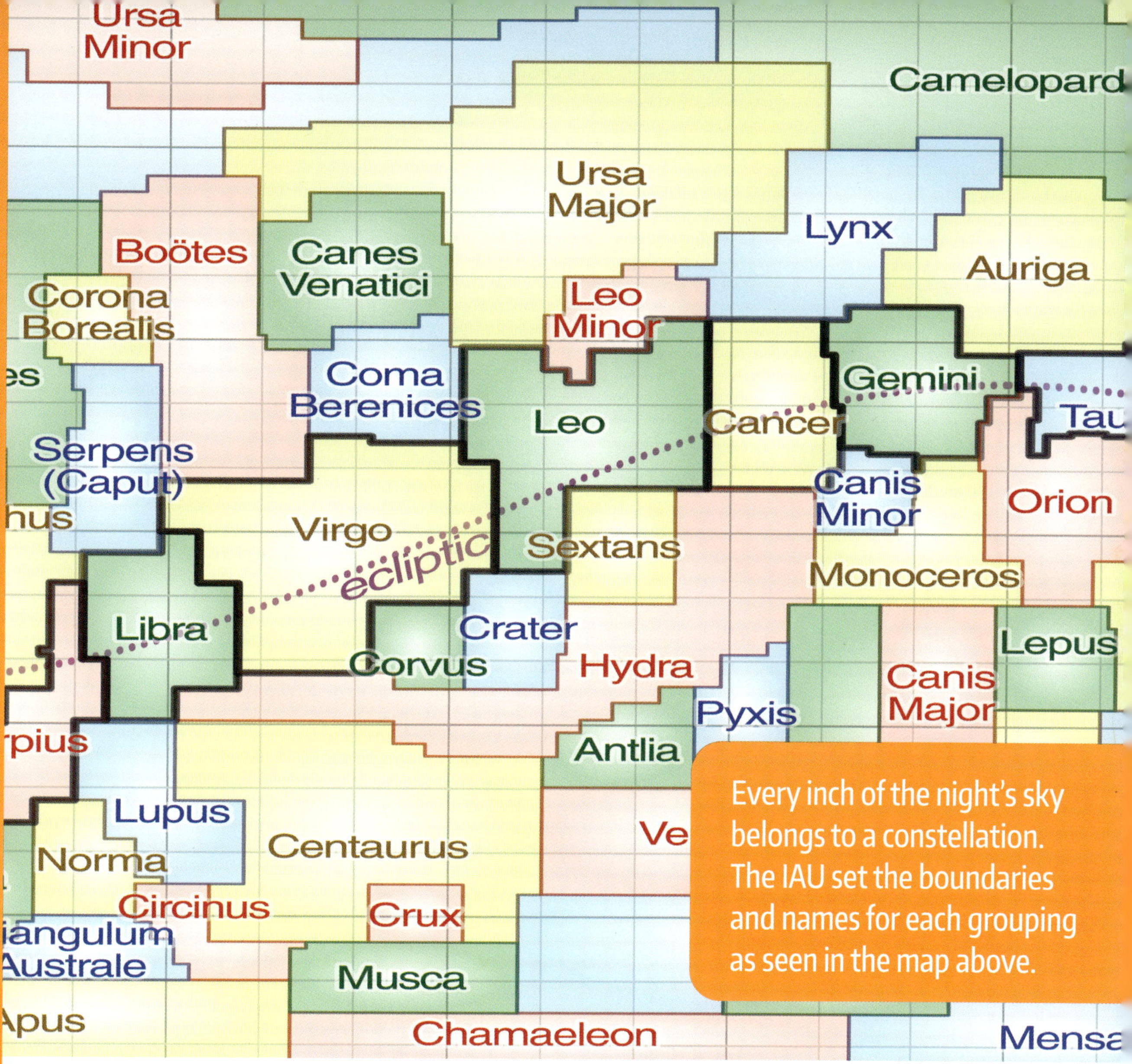

Every inch of the night's sky belongs to a constellation. The IAU set the boundaries and names for each grouping as seen in the map above.

Consider This

Maps of the sky are like maps of Earth. Instead of lines of latitude and longitude, though, the night's sky has lines marking right ascension and declination.

Hemispheres

Earth is divided into multiple **hemispheres**—Northern, Southern, Eastern, and Western. Whether you are in the Northern or Southern Hemisphere affects what you see in the night sky. Ptolemy lived in the Northern Hemisphere, so his list included only the constellations that he could see from there. He did not realize there were constellations he could not see.

The equator, an imaginary line around the middle part of the Earth, separates the Northern and Southern Hemispheres.

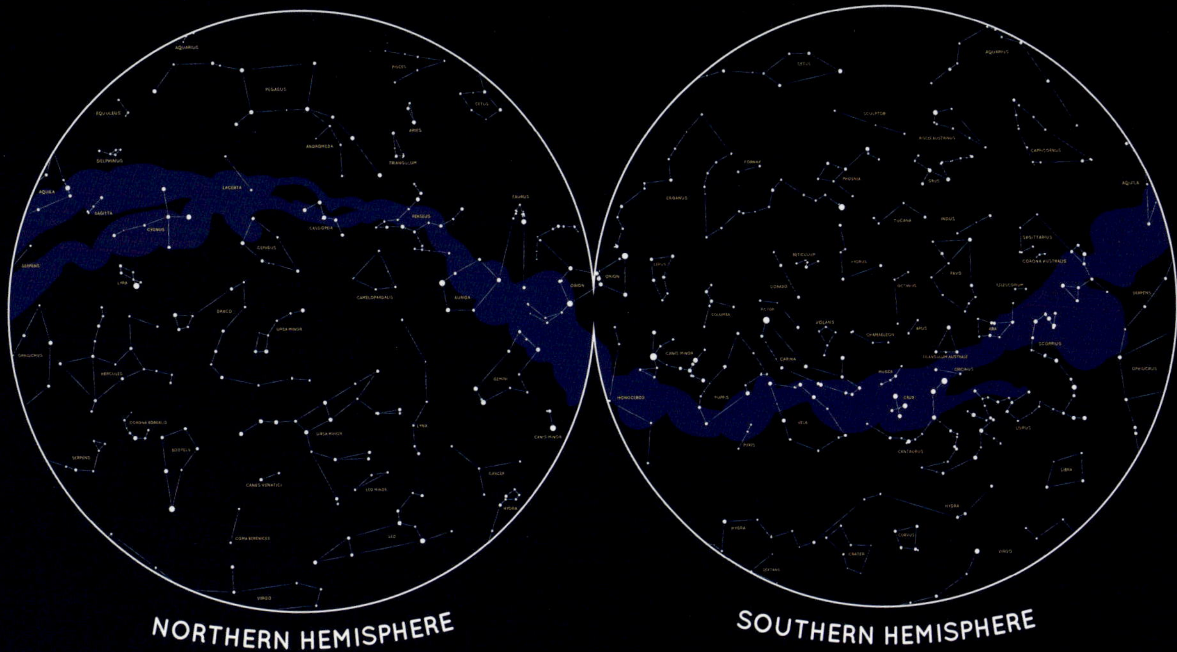

These star maps show how the night sky differs whether you're looking from the Northern Hemisphere or Southern Hemisphere.

Most constellations can be seen by people in both hemispheres, but not all. Depending on where one lives, different constellations appear at different times of the year. This is because Earth orbits the sun, and the view of the sky changes as Earth moves. The zodiac constellations are in the ecliptic, which is the path the sun takes as it crosses the sky throughout the year.

WORD WISE

THE WORD HEMISPHERE COMES FROM THE GREEK WORDS *HEMI* ("HALF") AND *SPHAIRA* ("SPHERE").

Spring Constellations

We see different constellations in the sky depending on not just where we are but the time of year. In spring, people who live in the Northern Hemisphere see the constellations Boötes, the Corona Borealis, and Cancer, one of the zodiac signs.

Boötes features one of the brightest stars in the sky, Arcturus. The shape of this constellation represents a man holding a spear, club, or staff, with two dogs nearby. The man is called "the herdsman." Different legends state he was the son of different gods.

The dogs to the right of the herdsman are part of a separate constellation called Canes Venatici, or the Hunting Dogs.

The name for the brightest star of Corona Borealis, Alphecca, comes from the Arabic name for the constellation.

The semicircular Corona Borealis, just to the left of Boötes, represents the story of Ariadne, a princess who was rescued from an island by the god Dionysus. He gave her a crown of jewels. When she died, the god threw the crown into the sky. In Latin, *corona* means "crown" and *borealis* means "northern."

Consider This

How can a constellation, like Boötes, have more than one legend?

Summer Constellations

A different set of constellations are more noticeable in the Northern Hemisphere during the summer, including Lyra, Cygnus, and Aquila.

The story of Lyra involves Orpheus, who played beautiful music to save his wife. The constellation is seen in the shape of a musical instrument called a lyre, which is like a harp. Lyra contains a bright white star called Vega.

This illustration shows the harp-like constellation Lyra to the right and the Cygnus, or swan, constellation in the center.

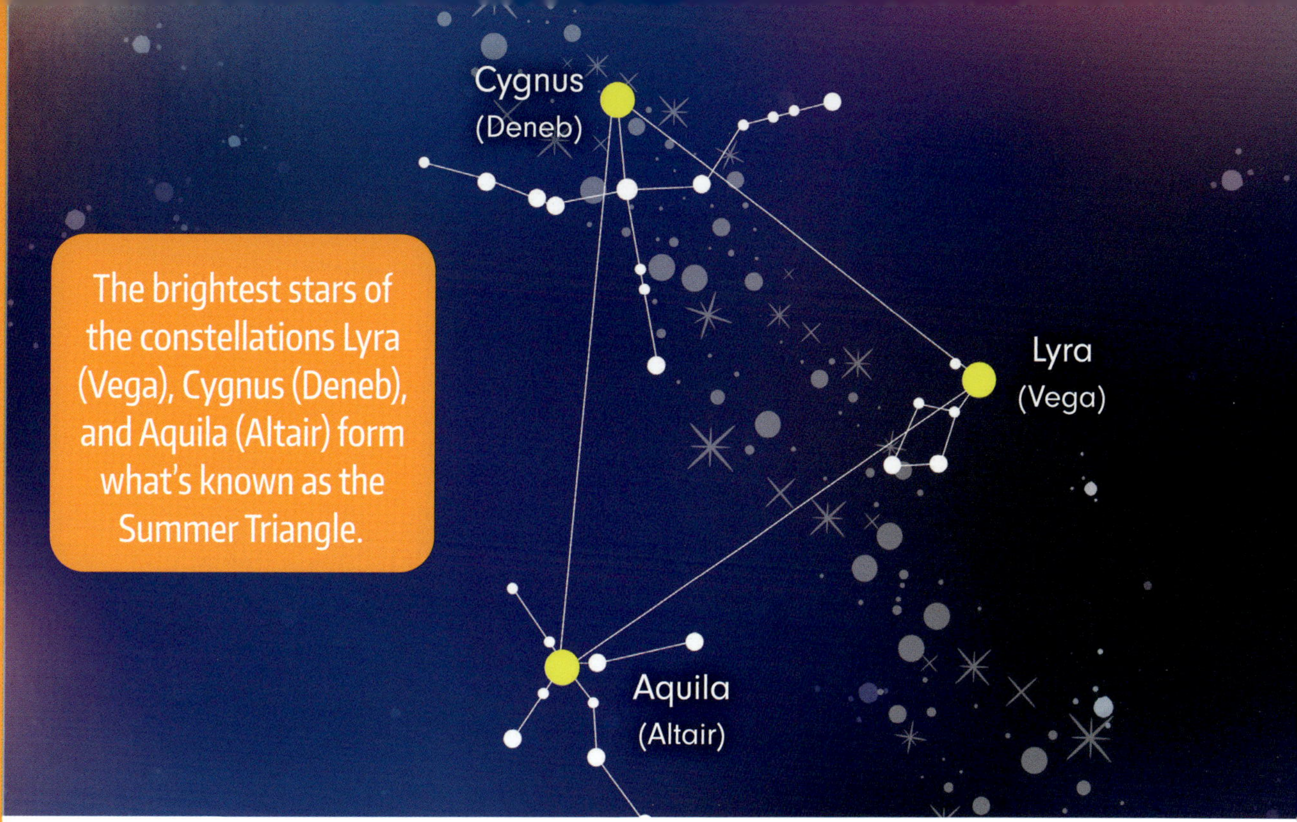

The brightest stars of the constellations Lyra (Vega), Cygnus (Deneb), and Aquila (Altair) form what's known as the Summer Triangle.

The constellation Cygnus, the swan, is also known as the Northern Cross. According to this story, the Greek god Zeus transformed into a swan to trick a woman into loving him. This constellation contains a very bright star called Deneb.

The constellation Aquila, which is Latin for eagle, represents the bird that carried the thunderbolts of Zeus. This constellation is found along a band of the Milky Way **galaxy**.

WORD WISE

A GALAXY IS A COLLECTION OF STARS AND PLANETS THAT ARE PULLED TOGETHER BY GRAVITY.

Fall Constellations

During the fall season, the Perseus and Pegasus constellations can be seen in the Northern Hemisphere.

A son of Zeus, Perseus was famous for killing the monster Medusa. Although Perseus can only be seen for part of the night in the summer months, every year in August a meteor shower seems to come from its northern stars.

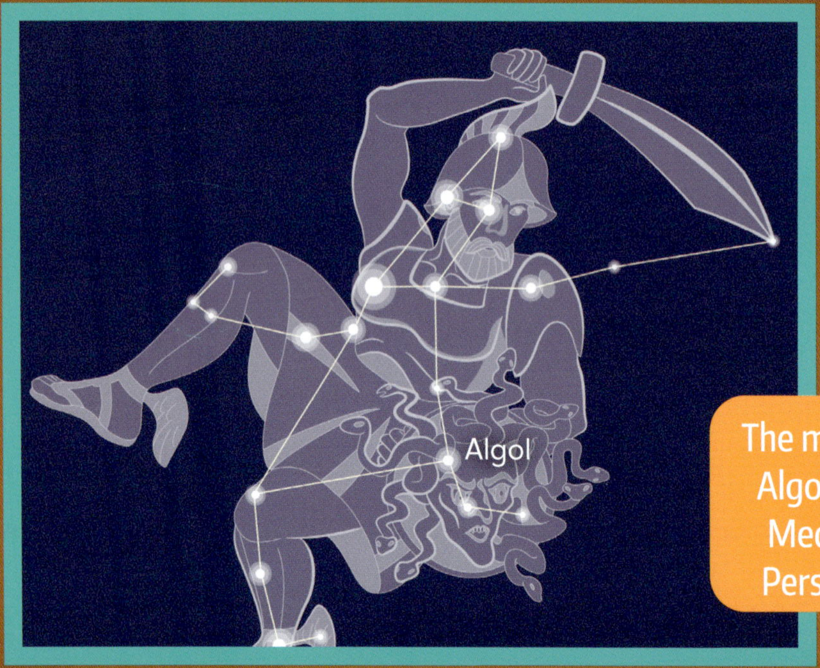

The multiple star system Algol makes up part of Medusa's head in the Perseus constellation.

When the smaller star, Algol Aa2, passes in front of Algol Aa1 from Earth's point of view, the light from the star system appears to dim. The smaller, third star, Algol Ab, is much farther away.

Perseus features Algol, the "demon" star. Ancient people feared the star because its light frequently changed in intensity. Astronomers now know Algol is at least three stars, one of which passes in front of another every few days, causing the change in light.

In mythology, Pegasus, the winged horse, went on heroic missions for the gods. The constellation looks like a square with three legs. Scientists made one of the first exoplanet discoveries around a star in this constellation, 51 Pegasi.

Consider This

As technology improves, what do you think astronomers will discover about the stars in constellations?

Winter Constellations

One of the most recognizable constellations in the winter sky is Orion. It appears in the Northern Hemisphere in the winter.

Orion, hunter for the gods, is the brightest constellation in the winter sky. Its upper stars represent shoulders, and the lower stars are legs. Two arms, one holding a bow, stretch up and out of the shoulders. Many people recognize Orion by the middle three stars, which look like the hunter's belt.

Orion has two dogs behind him—the constellations Canis Major and Canis Minor. Canis Major contains Sirius, the brightest star in the night sky. Canis Minor's brightest star is called Procyon. These two stars, combined with Betelgeuse in Orion, form what's known as the Winter Triangle.

The three stars that make up Orion's belt in the middle of this constellation are easy landmarks to see in the night sky.

compare and contrast

Which season do you think is the best for stargazing? What time of year would give you the best view?

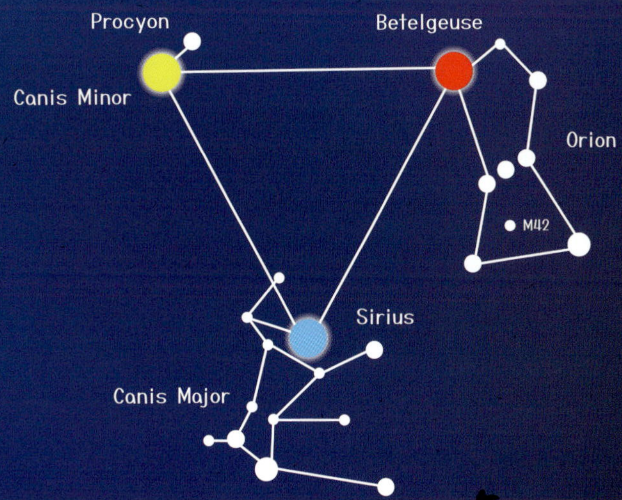

The brightest stars of the constellations Orion (Betelgeuse), Canis Major (Sirius), and Canis Minor (Procyon) form what's known as the Winter Triangle.

Glossary

astronomers Scientists who study space.
boundary Something that marks the edge of a space.
celestial Relating to the sky.
civilizations Well-organized and developed societies that demonstrate a commitment to art, science, and culture.
cultures Particular societies that have their own beliefs, ways of life, art, etc.
cylinder An object shaped like a can.
harp A stringed instrument with an arched neck and supported by a post.
latitude An imaginary line around Earth that tells how far north or south of the equator one is.
legends Stories from the past that are believed by many people but cannot be proved to be true.
longitude An imaginary line around Earth that tells how far east or west of the prime meridian one is.
meteor An object from space that creates a streak of light in the night sky when entering Earth's atmosphere.
navigation The act of finding the right direction.
nomads People who do not have a permanent home.
orbit The path taken by one body circling around another body.
sedentary Less physically active.
telescope A device used to see faraway objects in the night sky up close.

For More Information

Books

Bestard, Aina. *What's Hidden in the Sky? Animal Constellations Around the World.* Miami, FL: Tra Publishing, 2022.

Cock-Starkey, Claire. *Lore of the Stars: Folklore & Wisdom from the Skies Above.* Beverly, MA: Wide Eyed Editions, 2023.

Sabol, Stephanie. *Where Are the Constellations?* New York, NY: Penguin Workshop, 2021.

Websites

International Astronomical Union

www.iau.org

Visit the official website of the IAU to see the full list of all 88 constellations and information about their individual stars.

NASA Space Place: Constellations

www.spaceplace.nasa.gov/search/constellations

Explore photos, videos, and fun activities to learn about constellations on this NASA website.

Publisher's note to educators and parents: Our editors have carefully reviewed these websites to ensure that they are suitable for students. Many websites change frequently, however, and we cannot guarantee that a site's future contents will continue to meet our high standards of quality and educational value. Be advised that students should be closely supervised whenever they access the internet.

Index